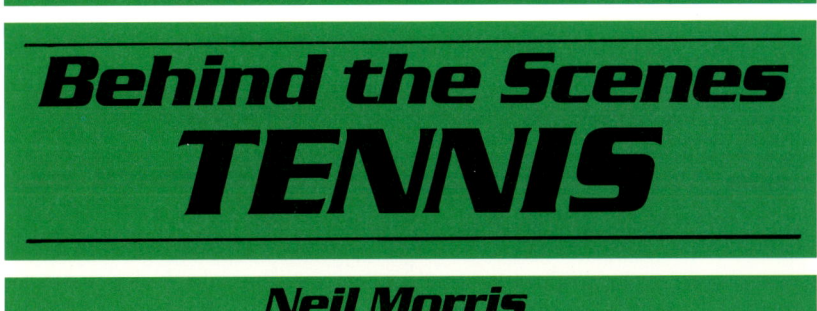

Behind the Scenes
TENNIS

Neil Morris

CHERRYTREE BOOKS

A Cherrytree Book

Designed by Les Dominey
Produced by
Autumn Publishing Ltd
Appledram Barns
Chichester, West Sussex

First published 1991
by Cherrytree Press Ltd
a subsidiary of
The Chivers Company Ltd
Windsor Bridge Road
Bath, Avon BA2 3AX

Photography Allsport UK Ltd

Line drawings by Carter Beatty,
West Sussex

With thanks to Ann Page (ITF)
for her assistance.

British Library Cataloguing in Publication Data
Morris, Neil
  Tennis.
  1. Lawn tennis
  I. Title II. Series
  796.342

  ISBN 0-7451-5113-2

Printed in Singapore by Imago Publishing Ltd

CONTENTS

Tennis around the world

Tennis is one of the most international of sports. It is played all over the world. As many as 159 countries are members of the International Tennis Federation and more than 30 of them stage international tennis tournaments and competitions every year.

Most people play tennis purely for enjoyment, relaxation or exercise, but some decide to make the game their career. Whether they compete alone in singles matches or with a partner in doubles matches, the aim of such players is to win and, in doing so, to earn enough money to keep on playing.

The world tennis circuit

The professional player who wants to play as many matches as possible can travel the world throughout the year. The world tennis circuit starts outdoors in Australia in January, and finishes indoors in Europe in December. On this world circuit, there are matches both for teams and for individuals.

In December 1989, Boris Becker led West Germany to a second successive Davis Cup triumph in Stuttgart. The victorious German team from left to right – Patrick Kuhnen, Boris Becker, Eric Jelen, Carl-Uwe Steeb and non-playing captain Niki Pilic.

Team events

Many players enjoy the companionship of a team event. When one team plays another, players can support each other without worrying if they will meet the next day on opposite sides of the net. At individual tournaments the finalists may be rivals for the match, but behind the scenes they are in fact good friends.

The Davis Cup is the most important men's team championship with about 90 countries taking part each year. Teams compete throughout the year with matches taking place at regular intervals and in different countries. The final is held at the end of each year.

A team of three or four men from one country plays a team from another country in a series of singles and doubles matches. The teams are divided into a World Group (which is made up of the top 16 countries) and four zonal groups – Europe/Africa A, Europe/Africa B, America, and Asia/Oceania.

World rankings

All professional players are ranked according to a points system that reflects their performance. At recognized tournaments only, players gain points that are fed into a computer, which works out the order in which they are ranked. The number of points each player gets depends on the type of tournament, which round the player reaches and the rank of the beaten opponent. Obviously, more points are gained for beating a high-ranking opponent.

Men players are ranked by the Association of Tennis Professionals (ATP) and women by the Women's Tennis Association (WTA). Both ranking systems calculate separate singles and doubles rankings and divide the number of points gained by the number of tournaments played to give an average over 52 weeks.

The ATP produces a new list of rankings and points every week, and the WTA produces their rankings every other week. There are over 2000 professional tennis players included in the two sets of listings.

After the first round of the competition, the losers in the World Group must play the winners from the zonal groups. The winners of these matches will be in the next year's World Group. This system allows every country a fair chance of winning.

The Federation Cup, which takes place for one week each year in a different country, is the women's equivalent of the Davis Cup. As many as 45 countries take part, playing qualifying rounds, preliminary rounds and then a straight draw. Again, this means that no country can be sure of success.

The Wightman Cup was a famous women's team event which took place every year between the United States and Britain. Early in 1990 it was suspended because the Lawn Tennis Association (LTA) of Great Britain felt that Britain was no longer able to make a match of it. However, it is to be revived as a competition between the United States and Europe.

Tennis was re-introduced to the Olympic Games in Seoul in 1988, after a gap of 64 years. Entries were decided by a country's performances in the Davis Cup and the Federation Cup. The result was many exciting matches and the acceptance of tennis as a worldwide sport.

Martina Navratilova (right) and her partner, Pam Shriver (both USA) – one of the greatest women's doubles partnerships of all time. Together they have won the doubles Grand Slam three times and they hold the record for winning 109 doubles matches in a row.

Individual tournaments

The men's ATP Tour and women's Kraft General Foods Tour tournaments are held all over the world and are played on a variety of surfaces.

A relatively new tennis tournament, the ATP Championships takes place in November as the climax to the Tour. The top eight players in the ATP rankings compete in this event.

The women's Tour is made up of 64 tournaments, the most important of which is the Virginia Slims Championships. These are held in America every year in November and are played out by the top 16 women players.

The Compaq Grand Slam Cup, created in 1989 to reward players who performed best in the Grand Slam championships, was contested for the first time in December 1990, in Munich, Germany. In this event, the 16 men with the best records at the Australian Open, the French Open, Wimbledon and the US Open, or two alternatives, compete in a direct elimination tournament.

Veterans' events

In these events players can compete in championships at virtually any age. There are international championships held all over the world, such as the Marble Cup for women over 60 years or the Crawford Cup for men over 70 years of age.

In 1988, Steffi Graf (GER) completed a 'Golden Grand Slam' when she won a gold medal in singles at the Olympic Games in Seoul. Steffi gained a world computer ranking at the age of 13 years, and at the same age won the German Junior Championships for Under-18s.

The tournament draw

When the list of players entering a competition is complete, the organizers do their best to make sure that the players are well matched. In a small tournament made up of 32 players, the organizers would probably automatically award places to the 24 players with the highest rankings. In addition, four places might be kept for lower-ranking players who would have to win through qualifying rounds. The last four places might be so-called wild cards which could be awarded, for example, to local players or to a famous player who is no longer very high in the rankings.

The draw is arranged so that the eight highest-ranking players, or seeds, as they are called, will not meet each other until the quarter-finals. If the two best players are unbeaten, they will meet in the final.

Ivan Lendl (USA) is seen here with the Australian Open trophy which he won in 1990 while ranked No.1. Lendl has won all the major championships except Wimbledon. A true professional both on and off the court, his determination saw him in the world's top 10 players throughout the 1980s.

Major championships

Top left: Some of the grass courts of Wimbledon, London.
Top right: An aerial view showing the crowds at Flushing Meadow, New York.
Bottom left: The 'court central' at Roland Garros, Paris, showing the red clay surface.
Bottom right: The Flinders Park complex close to Melbourne city centre.

The four major championships in the world of professional tennis are the Lawn Tennis Championships at Wimbledon, the US Open at Flushing Meadow in New York, the French Open at Stade Roland Garros, Paris, and the Australian Open at Flinders Park, Melbourne. It is the ambition of every top player to win these championships. If a player manages to win all of them in one year, he or she has completed a Grand Slam and is awarded a special trophy as it is such a rare achievement.

Wimbledon

The Lawn Tennis Championships at Wimbledon is the most famous tennis tournament in the world. Wimbledon's reputation has come a long way since its first tournament, held in 1877. At that time there were only a few hundred spectators. Now more than 400,000 people pass through the gates during the two weeks of the tournament, which starts at the end of June. Millions more watch Wimbledon on television.

New safety codes have been introduced to restrict the number of people entering the All England Club. Only 28,000 spectators are permitted in the grounds at any one time. In addition, there is no longer any standing room at the Centre Court, which holds 13,000 people.

Apart from the Centre Court there are 17 other grass courts and a further 12 for players to practise on. Wimbledon's grass courts give this tournament the unhurried, traditional, club-like atmosphere for which it is so famous. It is popular with players and spectators alike, and tennis enthusiasts apply for tickets several months in advance. The LTA, however, limits the number of tickets sold in advance to tennis clubs and private individuals. If people are not lucky enough to get tickets this way, they can buy cheaper tickets at the gates on the day – as long as they don't mind queueing!

Some Wimbledon records

Most singles titles:
Men : W C Renshaw (GBR) 7 times, 1881-6 and 1889.
Bjorn Borg (SWE) 5 times running 1976-80.
Ladies: Martina Navratilova (USA) 9 times, 1978-9, 1982-7 and 1990.

Youngest champions:
Boris Becker (GER) 17 years in 1985 (he was unseeded at the time).
Miss L Dod (GBR) 15 years in 1887.

Longest match:
Pancho Gonzales (USA) beat Charlie Pasarell (USA) in 5 hours and 12 minutes in 1969 (before the tie-break was introduced).

Shortest final:
Mrs R Chambers (GBR) beat Miss P Boothby (GBR) in only 25 minutes in 1911.

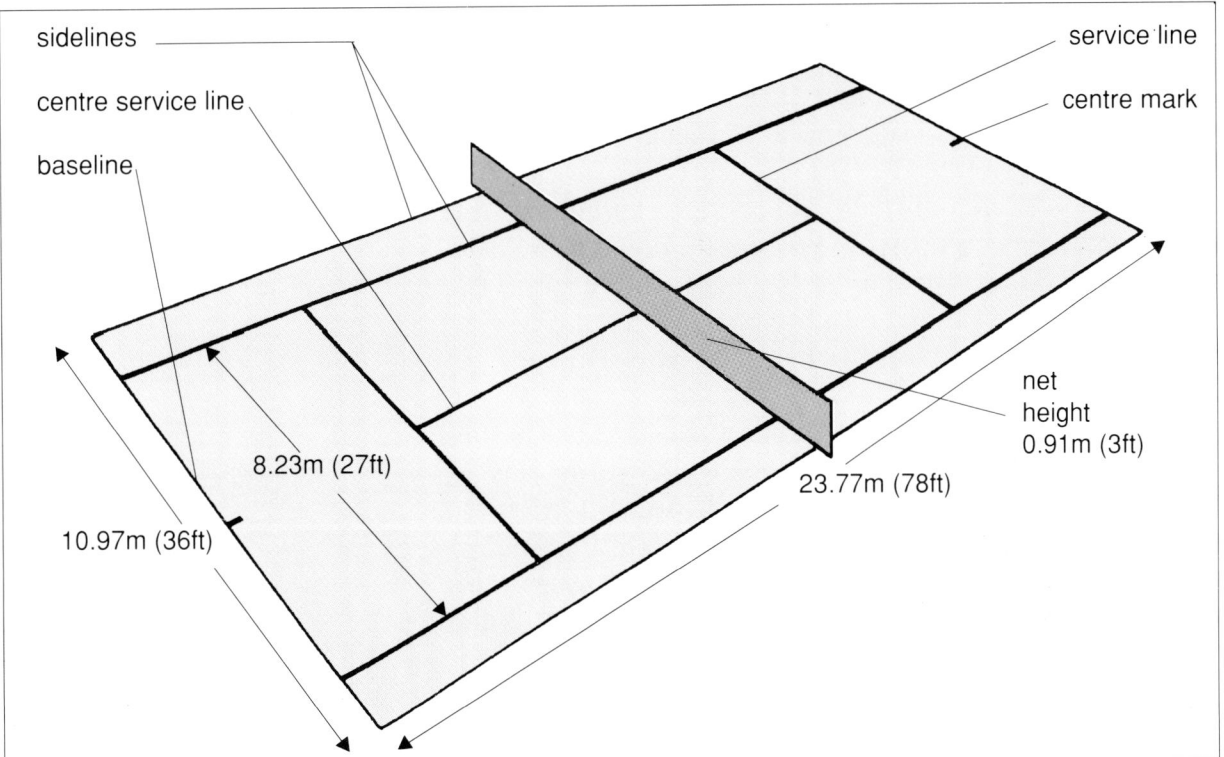

sidelines

centre service line

baseline

service line

centre mark

net
height
0.91m (3ft)

8.23m (27ft)

23.77m (78ft)

10.97m (36ft)

Tennis courts are marked following strict measurements.

The US Open

The atmosphere of the US Open, which takes place at the end of August at Flushing Meadow, is quite different from that of Wimbledon. The audience in the 20,000-seat Stadium Court tends to be much noisier. The constant roar of jets flying overhead and the smell of hamburgers and popcorn wafting around create an atmosphere that players either love or hate.

A problem for some players is the influence that television schedules have over the timing of the matches. Play starts at 10 am and may go on until after midnight. There are often long gaps between matches, and players are not always sure what time their next match will start. In order to ensure that the matches coincide with peak viewing times, many of them are played under floodlights. Bjorn Borg claims this is one reason why he never won the US Open.

In spite of this, very few top players miss the tournament. The computer points for the rankings are too important and the prize money too valuable to be ignored.

The French Open

Stade Roland Garros is a smaller site than any of the other Grand Slam locations. The centre court has an open arena that can hold about 17,000 spectators, and there are 15 other courts. The French Open is the most important tournament played on red clay. Although European players tend to do best on this type of surface, in 1989 the American player, Michael Chang, won the French Open. Not only is it unusual for an American to win this tournament, but Michael was only 17 years old at the time!

The tournament starts at the end of May, just before Wimbledon. Many players find the switch from clay to grass very difficult, so if they are beaten in an early round in Paris, they will often go straight to England to start practising on grass. Occasionally, top players miss this tournament altogether to give themselves more time to practise and so have as good a chance as possible of winning Wimbledon.

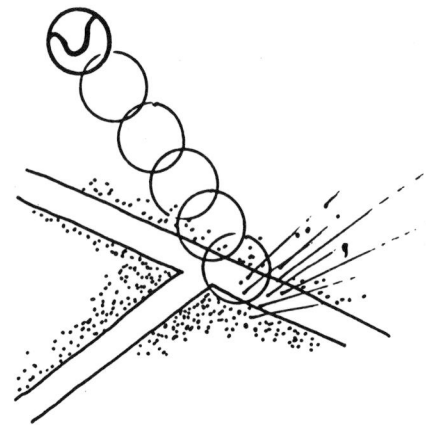

Sometimes it is almost impossible to tell if a ball is in or out. If it lands on a line, it is in. A line monitor beeps when a ball is out.

The Australian Open

The Australian Open, which starts at the end of December or beginning of January, is sponsored by the Ford Motor Company and is televised around the world. It is played at the Flinders Park National Tennis Centre which has 15 outdoor courts. The main feature of its Stadium Court is a retractable roof which is normally left open, but can be closed if it rains. Like Flushing Meadow in New York, Flinders Park is open to the public for the rest of the year, whereas both Wimbledon and Roland Garros are private clubs.

Courts and their upkeep

Each of the major tournaments is played on a different surface – Wimbledon on grass, the French Open on clay, the US Open on rubberized asphalt and the Australian Open on a cushioned hardcourt surface made of polyurethane and rubber. Each type of surface requires a different style of tennis. For example, balls spin and bounce low on grass so players tend to rush up to play at the net, while balls on cement and clay courts bounce higher and the players stay back at the baseline.

Players often slide into their shots when they play on a clay surface. This makes it necessary to rake and water the courts regularly.

The upkeep of each surface is different, too. Rubberized asphalt courts must be swept to clear loose bits; clay courts have to be raked and sprinkled with water every day; and grass courts need constant attention, even when not in use. When matches are being played at Wimbledon, court coverers stand by, ready to pull heavy covers over the courts when it rains. Particular care is taken with line markings on grass courts because the grass wears away and the lines become smudged.

Immediately after each Wimbledon fortnight, the grounds are prepared for the next year's Championships. The courts are repaired, and patches of worn ground are sown with new grass. Work continues on the courts all year round. They are looked after with great care by a head groundsman and eight assistants.

Coaches and managers

Professional tennis players depend on a number of people to help them in their quest for success. The two most important people are probably the player's coach and his or her manager.

Coaches

Anyone wanting to learn the game of tennis or improve their game can pay for coaching lessons. A coach will teach them the skills of the game and, if necessary, prepare them for the pressures of match play.

Top players, however, must have confidence in their coach's ability to help them when, and if, problems occur. No player has succeeded in the competitive world of professional tennis without the support of a coach they like and trust. The partnership must be one of co-operation: the player must be willing to listen to advice and the coach must be ready to understand the player's problems. This combination helps to produce a successful player. Coaches are often ex-players. Tony Roche, Ivan Lendl's coach, is a former world-class player. Stefan Edberg's coach, Tony Pickard, is a former British Davis Cup team player.

Some top players' coaches

Ian Barclay has coached Pat Cash since Cash was 11 years old. When he was 16, Cash was ranked No 342 in the world; at 22 he was No 7, reaching the final of the Australian Open and winning Wimbledon.

Craig Kardon has coached Martina Navratilova since December 1988; before this Martina had many coaches, including Mike Estep and Tim Gullikson.

In Kardon's first year with Martina she won eight tournaments and over one million dollars.

Pavel Slozil coaches Steffi Graf and so does her father, Peter; so Slozil has to please player and father.

Bob Brett has coached Boris Becker since December 1987. Becker is managed by former Rumanian professional Ion Tiriac.

A special relationship

Different players have different needs. A player and a coach develop a relationship that suits them best. Stefan Edberg, for example, may not see his coach for several tournaments but they will make detailed plans for Stefan's preparation for each of the events. Whenever John McEnroe felt that he was having problems with a particular shot, he would telephone his coach, Tony Palafax, in New York to talk the difficulty through.

Some players need to be helped mentally as well as physically. Bjorn Borg, for example, was very superstitious about preparation for a match. He would not shave during championships, and he would follow the same routine from the moment he got up in the morning until the time when he walked on to the court. His coach, Lennart Bergelin, would help him through this ritual, as well as preparing his match tactics against the player he was about to meet.

The French player, Henri Leconte (centre) and his coach, Patrice Hageleur (right), at the Britain v France Davis Cup match in September 1990. France beat Britain on this occasion and entered the 1991 World Group.

Big business

When a player is playing tennis full time and reaches a standard where advice is needed regarding sponsorship, or help with organizing travel to tournaments, he or she will employ a manager. A tennis player's talent is big business, and a player can earn a great deal of money if he or she is well managed.

A manager's job is to balance the demands of tournaments, exhibition matches, promotional appearances, travel and rest, so that the player can concentrate on playing. A manager decides which tournaments suit a player's skills. There is not much point in taking part in a tournament where the standard is too high. A player will feel discouraged if easily beaten and there will be little chance of winning any prize money.

Sponsorship

As a player becomes better known and more successful, it is up to the manager to secure sponsorship agreements. The first step is to get sponsorship for equipment. The manager makes an arrangement with leading sports manufacturers who pay the player to wear clothing or use equipment that has the company's logos or emblems on it. Tennis racquet manufacturers, for example, mark the strings of their racquets with a design so that everyone will recognize their make. Players sponsored by the company use stencils to re-ink faded designs. Top players can earn a lot of money from sponsorship.

Professional players

Once a player has taken on sponsorship and joined the professional circuit (the ATP Tour for men or the Kraft General Foods Tour for women) he or she is a professional player. The main difference between amateur and professional tennis players is that professionals make a living from tennis (playing, coaching and sponsorship agreements) whereas, generally, amateurs do not depend on tennis for their living.

Managers are usually paid a percentage of a player's earnings. There are vast amounts of money to be won in

Some examples of the logos used by top sports goods manufacturers.

Many of the lower-ranked players spend time running coaching clinics in order to pay for their tournament expenses. These clinics can be a very good way for young players to pick up tips and learn to play like professionals.

competitions – £230,000 for the men's singles winner at Wimbledon 1990, and £29,900 for a quarter-finalist, for example.

Well-known players may also receive money for playing in exhibition or demonstration matches.

Equipment and clothing

During the last 20 years, tennis-playing equipment and clothing have changed out of all recognition. Before 1970, all players used a wooden racquet, wore canvas shoes with rubber soles, plain white clothes, and they played either on a grass or asphalt court. In the early 1970s sports goods manufacturers realized that they could make a great deal of money from tennis equipment, so they began to research and develop new designs and materials.

Racquets

Originally, tennis racquets were made of wood and strung with natural gut produced from the intestines of sheep and cows. Now it is possible to buy a wide variety of types of synthetic string, and have racquets strung to order. Many sports shops have their own stringing machines, and players can ask for exactly the tension they wish. Most top-class players prefer slacker stringing when they play on grass courts so that they can get more spin on the ball; strings have to be tightened for play on hard courts.

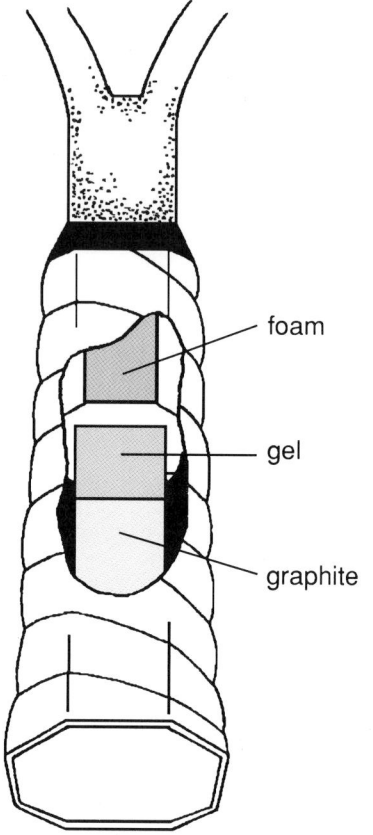

Some racquets have a section of gel in the handle that prevents shock waves from injuring a player's arm or wrist.

foam

gel

graphite

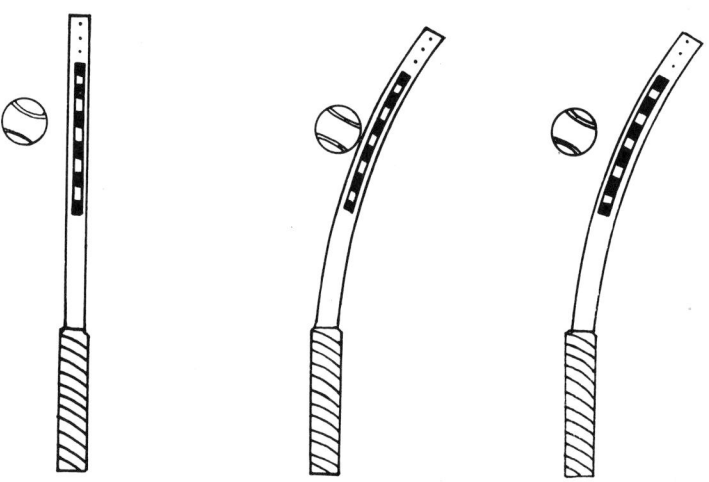

This illustration shows the effect of a ball hitting a racquet. Racquets are flexible and bend when a ball hits the strings. This happens too quickly to be seen by the naked eye.

Pressurized balls are used in tournaments. They have to conform to strict international rules of size, weight, compression and construction. They must be either yellow or white and stored at a constant temperature of 20°C.

Present-day tennis racquets are much lighter, stronger and longer lasting than the old wooden ones. Most racquets are made from a combination of different materials, such as graphite, fibreglass, boron and kevlar. Many of these materials were originally developed for the aerospace industry. As well as new materials, there are new methods of making racquets. For example, the racquet handle might have a case of aluminium alloy filled with graphite, with polyurethane foam under the grip. This gives players more power. It also protects arms and wrists from injuries that can come from the jarring shock waves caused by hitting a fast ball.

Balls

Tennis balls are now made in several bright colours. These are not a fashion accessory – it is simply easier to see the bright colours when playing. There are two types of ball, pressurized and pressureless. The pressurized balls have more bounce, but they wear out faster. The bounce of the pressureless, 'long life' balls depends on the material from which the core is made. They are very popular as practice balls.

Clothes

All players want to keep cool and be able to move freely, so a lot of women wear short skirts with T-shirts, or a tennis dress, and men wear shorts with a sports shirt or T-shirt. During practice and after a match players normally wear tracksuits. Top players may be under contract with a manufacturer to wear tracksuits with their logo or emblem at certain times and on particular occasions.

Footwear

Every year new and better designed shoes are developed. Professional players prefer leather-topped shoes which allow the foot to breathe, and various types of synthetic sole. It is important to have the right shoes for the right surface.

For players with a particular weakness the design of the shoes is very important. The correct shoe can protect or support any part of the foot or ankle that is particularly weak.

Socks are important too. To avoid getting blisters some players wear two pairs of socks. It is possible to buy special short socks for tennis, but whatever the style, cotton rather than synthetic fibre socks are more comfortable, as they allow the feet to breathe.

Official Grand Slam rules about sponsorship

Logos up to a size of 13 sq cm (2 sq in) are allowed as follows:

Shirt, sweater or jacket:
one manufacturer's logo on each sleeve, plus one extra logo on each; two manufacturers' logos on the front; logos on the back or collars of the shirt.
Shorts: two manufacturers' logos.
Socks/shoes: one manufacturer's logo on each sock and each shoe.

Racquet: standard logos of the manufacturer on racquet and strings.
Hat, headband or wristband: one manufacturer's logo without writing.
Bags, towels or other equipment: standard logos of tennis equipment manufacturer on each item, plus two commercial logos on one bag, neither more than 26 sq cm (4 sq in).

Left: Players no longer have to wear all-white clothes. Many clubs expect players to wear clothes that are mainly white and the same rules usually apply to tournaments. Stefan Edberg (SWE) won Wimbledon in 1990 wearing his own design of Adidas clothes.

Right: At the US Open in 1990, John McEnroe (USA) used sunblock to avoid sunburn. He was one of the first players to wear a headband. Nowadays, coloured strips of cloth are worn more as fashion accessories than for any practical purpose.

Accessories

Headbands became popular with players who had long hair, such as Bjorn Borg and John McEnroe. Although headbands were first worn for practical reasons, this trend became fashionable amongst sportspeople generally.

Another practical accessory are sweatbands which players wear on their wrists. Again, these have become fashionable amongst many sportspeople as well as tennis players. Logos and emblems also appear on sweatbands to promote sponsors' products.

Many players like to make their own grips for their racquet handles from brightly coloured synthetic strips. These grips absorb sweat and enable a player to keep a firmer hold on the racquet.

Making it to the top

Most coaches would say that the best players lay the foundations of their success between the ages of eight and 18, and are at their peak between the ages of 18 and 28 years. There are, of course, exceptions to this rule, such as Boris Becker or Steffi Graf, who reached the very top at a younger age. Or, at the other end of the scale, someone like Jimmy Connors, who ranked No. 1 in the world at the age of 21, won the US Open for the fifth time at the age of 30 and was still ranked No. 4 at 35 years old.

Very few players manage to stay at the top for longer than a few years, but Jimmy Connors (USA) is certainly an exception. He was top of the world computer rankings for three years from July 1974 to August 1977, and 10 years later he ranked No. 4.

Training schemes

Many countries run national junior schemes, where exceptional players are guided by experienced coaches. These schemes try to keep a balance between training and schooling, something which can be difficult for ambitious players to manage on their own. Czechoslovakia, France, Sweden and Germany all have very successful national schemes, and as a result have produced excellent players. Such countries are fortunate

The racquets may seem rather large for such small players, but it is never too soon to learn how to play tennis.

in receiving financial aid from their governments to cover the cost of running tennis academies.

America, which also produces a high standard of players, tends to rely on the college system, as well as its tennis academies. Many colleges and universities in America have excellent sports facilities and coaches, and students are allowed time off from academic work to concentrate on their sport.

Britain lags behind in this field, with the result that it has very few top-class players. In recent years, however, sports schools such as the LTA's School of Excellence at Bisham Abbey, have been set up to improve the situation. In addition, Britain's first Junior Tennis Centre was opened in 1990 and it is the model for a chain of 50 indoor centres to open in the forthcoming years.

Jennifer Capriati (USA), at the age of 13 years, was the youngest player ever to compete in the Wightman Cup. Aged only 14 years, Jennifer played Monica Seles (YUG) in the semi-finals of the 1990 French Open before being knocked out.

Practice sessions

Training programmes depend on the experience of each player. Players between the ages of eight and 18 years must be careful not to demand too much of their bodies. They usually practise for about an hour a day, attempting to correct a particular problem and adjust their game to playing on different court surfaces.

Successful young players do not train too hard as they get plenty of practice during their matches. However, as with the development of any skill, it is better to do some practice every day than to have one long practice session each week.

Competitive play

A young person who is physically and mentally ready for matches against unknown opponents will find that there is plenty of competition. The standard of play may vary in different areas, but most players start with club tournaments, followed by inter-club matches. Success at this level might mean a place in a regional or county team, or national junior tournaments where the country's best young players meet. There are many good players in regional tournaments, but very few manage to get over the next hurdle and arrive on the international circuit.

Top junior players aged from 14 to 18 years have

their own international circuit. There are more than 100 tournaments in over 60 countries, with a points and ranking system similar to the seniors'. Each of the Grand Slam championships has a junior tournament too, and there are team events similar to the Davis and Federation Cups.

Preventing burnout

Professional tennis players seem to be getting younger every year. To prevent young and enthusiastic players overstretching themselves, the Women's International Professional Tennis Council laid down a set of rules for girls entering events offering $10,000 (£5000) or more. The rules allow certain age groups to enter only a limited number of tournaments a year. For example, players of 14 to 15 years may compete in a maximum of 15 professional tournaments a year and those aged 15 to 16 years are allowed a maximum of 17 tournaments a year. Players under 16 years must have two 30-day rest periods during each year of competition. They must continue their education to the satisfaction of the national requirements in their country.

Although there are no official guidelines for boys, their coaches and managers will generally follow the same principles as those which apply to girls.

Zina Garrison (USA) reached the 1990 Wimbledon final by beating both Monica Seles and Steffi Graf. The youngest of seven children, Zina started playing tennis when she was 10 years old. She often visits schools to give talks and pass tips on to youngsters.

The life of a tennis professional

Are professional tennis players born or made? The answer is, probably a bit of both. Most of the best players are natural athletes who would have succeeded in another sport, but they decided to put all their skills and energy into the game of tennis. The stamina and athletic skills that tennis demands means that no amount of coaching could turn a mediocre athlete into a top-class tennis player. Even the best athletes who want to become professional tennis players have to work very hard indeed.

The champions' dance – an off-court tradition. For once, onlookers have the chance to see players in dinner jackets and dresses instead of their usual tennis kit.

Fitness

All players need to be extremely fit. They need to develop stamina, speed, strength and mobility. Stamina is built up by long-distance running, for example, a 30-minute run two or three times a week. Speed can be developed by a programme of short runs, changing direction around a tennis court. For strength, many players do circuit training and weight training to develop their muscles, and stretching exercises or yoga to help mobility. To build up strength in the hand that grips the racquet, players use strengthening devices, such as squeezing putty.

Any player, whatever their age and experience, must expect to do these types of exercise as part of a daily routine to keep themselves in top physical condition. Some players – Ivan Lendl, for instance – enjoy playing sports other than tennis. Lendl loves to play golf, and ice hockey, and cycles to build up strength in his legs.

Diet

Proteins, carbohydrates and vitamins should be the basis of a tennis player's diet. Proteins, which are found mainly in fish, meat and dairy products, build and maintain the body's muscles. Sugar and fats provide short-term energy, but this is not enough for the sustained energy needed in a tennis match. Carbohydrates, found in bread, rice, pasta, cereals and

Diamonds are forever

The trophy for the European Community Championship is the impressive 'Antwerp Diamonds' Cup.

It is a full scale gold tennis racquet, encrusted with diamonds, and is the richest and most distinctive of all the trophies on the circuit today. It is valued at $850,000 (£425,000). When a player has won the trophy for the third time he is allowed to keep it – Lendl, who has won four times since the start of this championship in 1984, has now got one safely tucked away in a US bank vault.

potatoes, are absorbed gradually by the body, so they are ideal for providing energy over a length of time. Tennis players often have a pasta meal the day before a match.

Fluid is vital during and after a strenuous match as players sweat a lot, and loss of body fluid affects their performance.

Travel and accommodation

The life of a professional tennis player is not all glamour and glory. Travelling takes up a lot of time and is tiring, too. During a tour, players probably compete in a couple of different countries each month. The women's tour, for example, takes them round the world, starting off in Australia in January and ending in Brazil in December.

In order to save time, players usually travel by air. However, crossing several time zones in relatively few hours causes jet lag and tiredness. This is why players plan their schedules carefully and never play in too many tournaments.

Living out of a suitcase is easier if you are near the top of the tennis ladder. Top players can afford to stay in

All professional players will suffer injury at some time in their career. When Kathy Jordan (USA) injured her right knee, she had to have surgery and spend a whole year getting back to fitness. Warming up and stretching muscles before play are the best ways to avoid injury.

hotels, and even to pay for family and friends. Most tournaments arrange hotel accommodation for the players, but for those lower down the rankings there is the problem of expense. Many of them stay with a family, which is obviously cheaper than a hotel. It can also be a more friendly stay. Although some players enjoy the more relaxed atmosphere, for those who like peace and quiet in order to concentrate on the matches ahead, staying with a family can be distracting and too noisy.

A player who is knocked out of a tournament early on and is not booked to play any doubles matches later in the week is expected to go home. This makes planning difficult, so players must be prepared to make quick decisions regarding travel and be capable of booking their own tickets. In contrast, the more successful players have a manager who books their flight home and pays their hotel bill.

Competing

Many players competing in Grand Slam events will be very nervous, no matter how many times they have played in them before. However, players try not to let their nerves affect their eating habits. Whether they suffer from butterflies or not, most players eat well a few hours before a match.

On the practice courts, players go through a series of stretching exercises to make sure their muscles are warmed up. Most players spend a further 30 minutes knocking up before they are ready to play.

An hour before the match, players go to the dressing rooms where they have a relaxing shower and a massage. Physiotherapists are on hand to check joints or muscles which may be giving trouble. A player with a weak knee, for example, may be advised to wear a support bandage during the match.

Just before a match, when players leave the dressing room, they are introduced to their opponents. Then it is time to go out onto the court together.

Once on the court, there is a toss-up to see who serves first and then five minutes to warm up. During these minutes players like to practise a few volleys, lobs

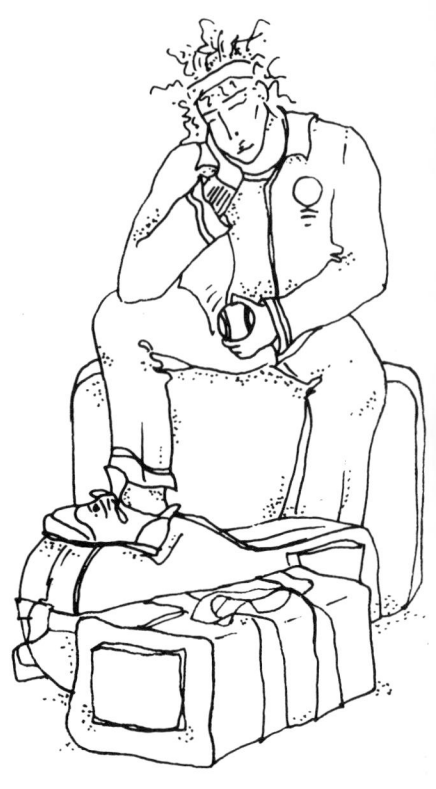

Life for a tennis professional is not all glamour. Too much travelling and too many tournaments will leave a player exhausted.

and serves, as well as their basic groundstrokes. The umpire keeps an eye on his watch and calls out to the players when the five minutes are up.

During the match, the changeovers between every other game last 90 seconds. In this time players can sit down, have a drink and freshen up. They are not allowed to receive any advice from their coach during the match.

The feelings of exhilaration, joy and relief when a professional tennis player wins a championship are witnessed and appreciated by thousands of people who watch tennis live or on television.

However, it is not necessary to have crowds of people watching, and press and television cameras present, to experience the sheer pleasure of winning a game of tennis. All players, no matter what age or standard, can congratulate themselves when they know they have played well and enjoyed the game.

A win is still a win, even at the lower tournament levels. If young players can 'learn to win' at lesser tournaments, they may go on one day to win a top event. Eric Jelen (FRG) won the Bristol Trophy in 1989.

INDEX